What's Your Business Worth?™

The entrepreneur and advisor's
guide to discovering, monitoring,
and optimizing business valuation

R꓀THINK PRESS

First published in Great Britain 2016
by Rethink Press (www.rethinkpress.com)

Praise

'Business Valuation has been a dark art practised sparingly by CPAs and chartered accountants for a high price point for business owners. Now, with the advent of Big Data, BizEquity has democratized it for the masses. This book is a great guide to help serve business owners and their advisors.'

Clarence Davis, former COO American Institute of Certified Public Accountants

'Most business owners will depend on the sale of their business to fund their retirement yet many don't know how much their business is worth. Business valuation has been disrupted by BizEquity empowering business owners with the tools to easily understand the value of their business.'

Jeffrey Fleischman, CMO, Penn Mutual.

'Business Valuation knowledge is the biggest data you need to know as an entrepreneur.'

Bill Shaw, VP Innovation, Entrepreneur Media

'We have chosen to partner with BizEquity as a means to provide business owners with a fast, efficient, inexpensive, and accurate way to know the value of their business.'

Rod Bazzani, VP Insurance, Equifax

'If you are like the 10 million baby boomers looking to sell in the next eight years, you need to know what you are worth today to succeed tomorrow. Now you can through this book and this service.'

Admiral Thomas Lynch, Chairman, New Day USA

This book is dedicated to Miles Frost, Co-Founder of Frost Brooks Partners and former lead Director of BizEquity. Miles and his investment partner Peter Brooks saw the possibility in BizEquity and helped the company to grow to be the market leader by leading our first institutional investment round. Miles tragically passed away while training for a marathon. He lived life perfectly. He was a true gentleman, friend, and business partner.

Miles will be sorely missed by everyone he met and touched by his good nature and good will. The expression 'time heals all wounds' is an unfair one when related to Miles, as you don't want to ever let time help you forget his passion, his integrity, his kindness, his intelligence, and his genuine nature.

Miles, you are the best and no one will ever forget you. You are our partner on this journey.

Mike and Dan

All profits from this book will be donated to the Miles Frost Fund, a charity set up to help to provide testing and diagnosis for hypertrophic cardiomyopathy (HCM) https://www.bhf.org.uk/ miles-frost-fund.

Contents

Introduction

If you own a business, it's probably one of your most valuable and prized assets. If you advise people who own businesses, don't underestimate you're dealing with "their baby" and you better know what you're doing or you won't be advising this client for long.

Knowing the value of a business can change the life of a business owner – especially over time.

If a property developer has access to property valuation data, they make better decisions and build more wealth over time. If a CEO has access to their share price valuation data, they make better decisions and build more wealth over time. It's no different for the millions of small and medium size business owners – knowing valuation data equals better decisions and more wealth.

Perhaps you don't know the worth of your business or your clients businesses. Maybe you're afraid of what it will show. Maybe you don't have the spare $7,500.00 oor the four weeks it traditionally takes to focus on an offline business valuation assessment.

Until recently, no software or service that could help you understand your value in a fast, simple, and cost effective way existed. As a result, 98% of all businesses on the planet have not been independently valued.

Think about it: there are software apps that tell you the value of your car, your house and your lawnmower but nothing that helps you to understand the value of the most important asset for many people – the value of their business.

That has all changed now, with the launch of BizEquity. Access to valuation data is a revolution for privately held businesses; it has already affected the lives of small business owners and their advisors.

In this book, I've brought together some of the best minds I know to share their knowledge. It is my pleasure to co-author this book with two good friends and colleagues who happen to be two of the smartest people I know in the area of business value; best-selling author Daniel Priestley is well known for the brilliant entrepreneurial insights that he shares with his legion of social media followers and readers; and Scott Gabehart is one of the most recognized experts on business valuation, and the author of *The Business Valuation Book*.

We have written this book to help you be able to answer the most important question you will ever be asked, or help your clients answer:

'What is your business worth?™'

Until recently, that question has been very difficult to answer for 99% Of all businesses, usually the smaller ones. A big business can look at their stock price or afford a large Wall Street or City of London investment bank to help it figure out its value, but for the over-200-hundred-million global small businesses a valuation was out of reach.

We at BizEquity have a mission to democratize this knowledge so that anyone, within minutes, can answer that million-dollar question. We have spent our professional careers and thousands of hours trying to break down the essential elements of what makes a business valuable, so that we could codify it and make a science out of what once was a dark art that was expensive, time intensive, and intrusive. We have codified it by making it the only patented and easy-to-use online-based software service that can help you understand your or your client's value.

Built for the 99%, not just the 1%.

Charlie 'Tremendous' Jones is quoted as having said, 'You will be the same person in five years as you are today except for the people you meet and the books you read.'

We hope that this book becomes one of those for you on your entrepreneurial journey.

All the best!

Michael M. Carter
CEO BizEquity

1

The Entrepreneurial Journey

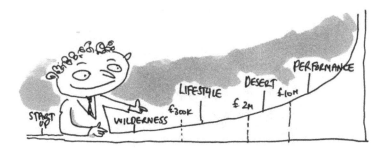

In order to begin answering *'What's your or your client's business worth?'* it is useful to explore where you are today. Entrepreneurship is a journey, and it's a lot more predictable than you'd think. There are phases that nearly every growing business goes through. Daniel Priestley (entrepreneur and best-selling author) describes the journey in six key stages:

Start-Up

These are the early days, when you have had your great idea, worked out how you are going to get started, and are preparing to launch your business. You are developing its offering, setting up an office, hiring the first staff members, and securing some funding for the journey ahead. Most businesses are funded by their founders, who should be thinking about how much it is worth now, and how much it will be worth in the future if all goes according to plan.

The
ENTREPRENEUR
JOURNEY

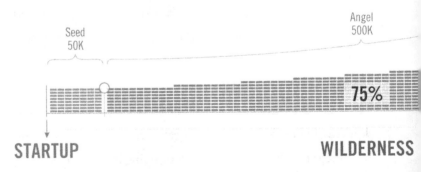

A start-up isn't typically worth much money outside its vision, its plan and its founders, but it's a healthy practice to think about valuation from the beginning.

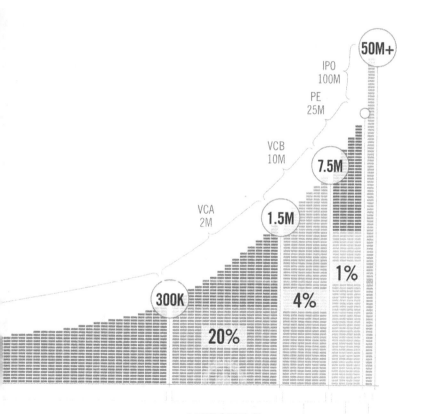

LIFESTYLE   DESERT **PERFORMANCE** UNICORN

A start-up can project where it will be in the future and then determine what the business will be worth when it gets to that point. Some start-ups have entered their projections into the BizEquity system and used the projected valuation to demonstrate the course they are on. Some have used their future valuation to adjust their initial plan.

If you had a plot of land and were considering building on it, would you want to know what the end result would be worth? Naturally you'd want to know the difference between building a large house, an apartment block or a commercial office. In the early stages, you can easily make changes and set up a construction that provides the best return.

It's the same with your business. In the early stages you can choose to focus on retailing direct to clients, wholesaling to resellers, providing a service, or developing a product. All of these decisions will lead to a different valuation, and it's worth knowing this in advance.

The Wilderness

Over 70% of all businesses in the Western world are very small and carry on in survival mode. Working with teams of one to three people, they have low overheads and often sell their own time or broker someone else's products. These business owners are usually self-employed individuals, and they rarely believe they have a scalable business. They are satisfied if they can meet their bills and make some more on top to allow them to live reasonably well. Making money by selling the business is usually far from their minds mostly because, without a real and accurate valuation, they don't believe they can.

These small operations sometimes sell for a small multiple of income. Occasionally you can sell a business like this or swap the shares for a stake in a bigger business. A focus on building valuation will be one of the keys to moving out of survival mode and into the next phase of business.

A very small business gets stuck in the wilderness because of a lack of direction and a perceived risk in expanding. The owner might really want to hire an extra person but be fearful of what it'll cost in both time and money. With additional information and some guidance they might gain the confidence and direction to expand.

A business valuation can lead to job creation, innovation and growth for these small businesses. It can be the catalyst to press ahead beyond a month-to-month existence.

Lifestyle Businesses

These are small but dynamic teams of 3-15 people who punch above their weight. These businesses have gone beyond survival mode because they have regular clients, intelligent marketing and sales programs, intellectual property assets and a vibrant culture. Often they choose to stay small and sometimes turn down opportunities so that they can stay lean. In many cases the owners would describe their business as their primary asset, other than their home.

A lifestyle business is where a value begins to emerge. Other people want what you have – the very essence of valuation. You'll also attract partnership opportunities, investors and employees who are motivated to build the value of the business if they are included.

A lifestyle business often has lots of potential. The business is typically sitting on fresh ideas, lean overheads and a dedicated team. It's well placed to expand if the owners want to. A valuation can help the business take on some investment, reinvest its capital sensibly, do an acquisition or structure an incentives program.

The Desert

Some business owners have grand visions for their future. They are determined to scale up, they want to push hard to grow, and to become a professional organisation. During the scaling stage, the staff typically grows from 15 to 50 people, but many of these businesses are not actually profitable, or cash flow becomes an issue. Any spare cash is often sucked into the growth engine of the business.

It's easy to become disheartened at this stage, when all the hard work doesn't seem to be paying off and all you can see is the bank balance. Even when the business is growing, the journey is lonely, hard and offers very few rewards during this phase.

When a business goes into this scale-up phase there's often little cash, longer payback cycles and a number of other challenges that emerge. A valuation is very important for many reasons: for one, it can motivate you or your client to keep going, knowing how profitable the return on investment will be later on. It can also help you keep your options open with regards to investment, acquisitions, mergers and employee incentives.

Performance Businesses

These businesses grow to be composed of over 50 people, with millions of dollars in revenue and healthy profit margins. They are successful, vibrant and valuable. They have a team, a culture and a brand that keeps attracting good clients and staff. These businesses have very valuable assets, and their valuations tend to represent life-changing amounts of money for the owners.

These performance businesses are starting to resemble grown-up companies. In the early days, a variety of people joined the business and enthusiasm was the key criterion for hiring (often without any real job description). Now the business has a human resource division that hires qualified executives to do work that is more clearly defined.

Part of being grown-up is dealing with banks, lawyers, accountants, insurers and investors who will all have something to gain from whatever business they manage to get out of you. At every turn people will talk about your financials and often reference your valuation, and if you yourself don't have an accurate idea of what your business is worth, it will be tempting and easy during negotiations and discussions to be swayed by the safest or most optimistic options presented to you. This only makes it even more essential that you have an objective and up-to-date business valuation efficiently carried out.

When you've crossed the desert and you have a performance business, you sure as heck better get some tangible rewards. Your valuation should help cure the after-effects of all those sleepless nights that came before.

When you use the BizEquity™ tools you'll notice that when a business hits a certain size (often US$10M+), the valuation seems to be disproportionately bigger. Our algorithms draw upon a lot of data which suggest that performance businesses are more valuable dollar-for-dollar than their smaller counterparts.

BizEquity™ can help you discover, monitor and optimize the value of your performance business.

Unicorns

Every industry has its outliers. These businesses break from all the normal trends, which is what makes them newsworthy. They grow super fast, and are acquired for amounts of money that seem ridiculous to most people. Just as it is foolish for an actor to base their plans on becoming an A-list Hollywood star, it's important for you not to base your expectations on these untypical and unpredictable examples. If you happen to be in the right place at the right time, and you have shares in a unicorn then you'll probably already know it was luck as well as prowess that made it happen.

If you have a unicorn business like WhatsApp, Uber, Facebook or Snapchat we probably can't help you, because you've got something that doesn't fit into very many boxes. Maybe you'll sell for a cool billion, or maybe Google and Apple will fight it out and end up paying you the GDP of Barbados. Whatever the outcome, the last thing it will be is predictable, and at BizEquity we are all about data and predictability.

Broadly speaking, these are the common stages of a business as described by thousands of people all along their business journey. Obviously not every business follows these stages exactly, but this is a useful way of separating the stages of business growth. There are highs and lows. Some people have the vision and the tenacity to keep going, others get disheartened, get stuck or give up. But nothing keeps people going like the knowledge that, despite the turbulence, they have created a company that is worth money. This knowledge allows them to evaluate what they have developed, measure what they have created, and to make informed decisions about the future of their asset.

You *will* exit your business

Wherever you are now on the Entrepreneur Journey, one way or another you're going to exit your business.

There are many different ways companies move on, and some ways are much more profitable than others.

Many pass their business on to their family. Some people sell to their management team.

Some get bored, some get divorced, some get old and some go bust. Some businesses live longer than their founders and are inherited.

There are people who have a business that doesn't take up a lot of their time, and so they exit from the day-to-day operations. Some business owners sell their business piece by piece.

Quite a few people sell for a small amount of money, and let others think they cashed out for a small fortune, while in reality they were barely able to clear their personal debts.

Most business owners will exit their business by closing it down and paying for the privilege – an accountant, a lawyer or a finance professional.

Some owners – fewer than most people think – plan their exit carefully and leave on their own terms. This allows them to sell their business for a lot of money and a better life.

Just as every business was once a startup, every business will eventually end.

Few start a business wanting to make money. A large portion of the money that can be made from a business is in the value of the shares when you sell them. The most important question you will ask when that time comes is: 'What's my business worth?'

The answer will affect the rest of your life. You may never have to work again, or you might need to go and get a job as soon as possible.

The worst time to find out your valuation is at the negotiation table.

It is therefore useful to address this question regularly, probably every month, so that when you sell, there are no surprises.

The valuation question is certainly one of the most important questions a successful public company CEO asks regularly. They know that it is the one that makes all the difference to their career and to the stakeholders.

The biggest companies in the world obsess over this question. CEOs of publicly traded companies can tell you their share price on any given day; almost all commercial decisions at a strategic level are asked within that context. Warren Buffet believes it is the most important question every business owner should address.

Ten years ago it would have been impossible to write this book for small business owners. Small businesses did not have access to the benefits that technology has now made available to them. Today, business and technology have come together to provide business owners with a new and valuable opportunity that allows them to take decisive action and maximise the value of their businesses.

This book will show you why answering the Valuation Question is the biggest key to building a valuable business. It is essential reading for entrepreneurs and business owners; to show you how to find out what your valuation is right now, how to improve it and how to plan your eventual exit.

It is not academic or highbrow. It is written to point you in the right direction so you can take the next steps, armed with all the information you need. It will give you your starting point so you can plot your end point.

To cut a long story short, you will need to get a valuation now if you want to maximize your valuation later. You will want to monitor your valuation over time too.

Why don't people get their business valued?

Many people think that they have a rough idea of what their business is worth, and that will do. It won't. Not if they want to make realistic, well-informed and, above all, profitable decisions at any time in the life of their company. The Million-Dollar Question, quite literally in many cases, is *How much is my business worth?*' And many business owners avoid asking it, preventing themselves from being able to answer it.

There are many reasons for this.

Most people are emotionally involved with their business – it is their baby – and they fear that they may find out that it is not worth very much. They also can find it very difficult to consider changing control or selling it, and accepting that they will have to step back. Sometimes what holds them back is just the logistics, costs or not knowing where to start.

Although everyone is aware that they need to make plans for the future, there are some uncomfortable facts that need to be faced, which many people prefer to ignore. Legacy planning is something that many people choose not to think about – often until it is too late.

Passing on a business to the family may be something that owners have always assumed they will do, but this assumption may not be met with the enthusiasm the business owners feel is appropriate. Business owner parents, for example, may find that their children want to build their careers in very different fields. This means that expectations have to be changed, and arrangements made for it to be sold to people who are unconnected with the family.

For businesses established by couples, the possibility of divorce puts both parties in an uncomfortable situation. Divorces are never comfortable, and valuing a business – often a couple's largest asset – adds to the discomfort between separating couples who have to share the value of something they have worked on together for years.

Reasons for Avoiding a Business Valuation (Until Now)

Cost: A valuation historically cost $8,000/£5,000 or more. Most small business owners don't have this sort of money to spend on something that doesn't give an immediate payback.

Privacy: The information used to construct a valuation is considered by many to be confidential. Passing all these figures to a stranger, and giving them that much insight into a business, can feel uncomfortable for business owners.

Discomfort: An accountant or similar auditor will need to poke around the business and ask some awkward questions. The staff might even start to wonder what's going on. Having to carry on with business as usual while this is happening could be a challenge.

Time: It's concerning for most business owners that it may take several weeks to get their business valuation. They imagine it to be a long-winded process that involved gathering and analyzing mountains of paperwork, and dozens of meetings and phone conversations.

Discounted Cash Flow (DCF) Based Models: Only valuing a business based upon DCF will underestimate the value of the millions of tax efficiently run businesses. Small businesses and their advisors think using publicly listed methodologies to value their private business will do the job. For most it won't.

Accuracy: After all the hassle, the information might not be accurate. And getting a second opinion would be tedious and expensive. So how would you even know?

Impartiality: A neutral third party is normally essential for a trusted valuation, and this means finding a new provider outside your usual suppliers. But even then, it's a lot of trust to put on someone, and there's always room for human error.

Information regarding valuing a business is often difficult to find, and frequently inaccurate. Most people believe that the process takes time and money, and is generally intrusive and uncomfortable. It must be neutral, conducted by a disinterested, professional and trustworthy third party, and how do you find one of those? They read articles in business magazines, or go by other people's referrals and experiences. Then, more often than not, they come to the conclusion that it is not worth all the trouble, effort and expense.

Wrong!

A valuation is the most important piece of information a business can have. And BizEquity can make sure you have it at your fingertips. Painlessly, and based on real world data, validated by experts. You will be equipped to move on with your business in any way you choose, knowing that you are well-informed and able to hold your own with investors, internal and external stakeholders, family members, and divorcing or separating partners of all kinds.

Valuing a business with BizEquity

Cost: $499 a year or free from your local financial advisor or banker if part of the BizEquity Network.

Time: Less than 10 minutes if you have your business data handy.

Intrusion: Totally private, simple, online, and confidential.

Accuracy: BizEquity is the world's leading provider of small-

and medium-sized business valuations, and draws upon over 100 million data points. We feed information from hundreds of external data providers ranging from real life business sale transactions; capital or debt financing data; to comparability ratios and learnings from millions of private businesses in our proprietary database. We also get client feedback that our reports are the useful tools they need to get alignment in deals and transactions every day.

Impartial: BizEquity is a global platform that has valued more companies than any other online valuation platform – 29.3 million and counting.

Your decisions will be based on current and powerful data.

2

The Story of BizEquity

Courtney Jones, a friend of Mike Carter's and the founder of the first publicly traded internet search company, findwhat. com, always says:

'Every great and important company ever created on earth has a creation story.'

This is BizEquity's.

The journey began in 2010, and today we're the global leader in business valuation, having valued over 33 million businesses.

Mike spotted a major opportunity to help businesses and business advisors all over the world to discover their value. Six years ago, there were categories of software for many inconsequential tasks, yet no category of software to help business owners answer the most important question they could ever answer:

'How much is my business worth?'

Michael Carter had been working for legendary investor Pete Musser for a number of years. His role was to identify opportunities across the United States, work with the entrepreneurs to structure growth capital, and to invest in some of the best and brightest ones.

In upstate New York, near Buffalo, he was looking at a company making lithium ion batteries. He asked the business owners, John and Gary, what they thought their business was worth. They looked at each other, shrugged and both said 'I don't know, roughly two times.'

Not bad, he thought. Twice revenue is a good start to a conversation.

Then they explained that they meant two times *earnings*. Wow, he thought. How can they think their business was only worth two times earnings when comparable companies were selling or trading at two to six times sales or revenue, and 10-14 times earnings?

He was fascinated that two relatively successful businessmen were completely ignorant of this fundamental knowledge.

He has learned the business from Pete, who always took a long-term view of partnership and centred everything on what it means to be fair to the entrepreneur and having integrity.

And on integrity.

He was therefore never going to take advantage of this valuation knowledge arbitrage.

Mike boarded the small US Airways commuter flight back to Philadelphia, thinking 'How is it possible that these two shrewd businessmen did not know what their business was worth? If they weren't in Buffalo, but in Boston or Brussels, they would have known its value.'

Maybe the network of advisors (accountants, wealth advisors, insurance agents, business consultants, bankers) in their market simply didn't know either, so they couldn't advise them.

This led to another, more significant question: 'How can 200 million people find out the value of their home through sites like Zillow or Zoopla; the value of a new or used car from TruCar or Kelly Blue Book, but not the value of their biggest asset?'

Clearly this was a major problem – and a terrific opportunity.

Mike didn't immediately know how it would be a business, but knew he had to democratize this knowledge and make it accessible to the people who needed it most: the small business owners. If Google could index the world's information, he wanted to index the value of every business around the globe. If he could do this, he was certain it could work as a business, because it was built on an important mission.

It didn't take him long to learn that John and Gary were not alone. Fewer than 2% of all business owners or businesses conduct a business valuation each year.

He also learned that

• valuation was a nearly $8 billion-dollar business in the U.S. alone, wherein only some 20,000 providers took up to four to six weeks, and charged \$8,000 (£5,000) to deliver a report offline (*IBIS World*).

- 40% of business owners don't have life insurance, and 50% of businesses are under-insured because they don't think their business has value, don't know how to find out, or don't have the resources to do so.

- nearly all wealth advisors producing a financial or estate plan for business owners or entrepreneurs don't have a simple and effective way to relate business assets and/ or ownership percentages in private companies to the annual estate plan. Thus they might be not optimally weighting, making the most of their portfolios, or doing the right planning for their clients.

- over 70% of businesses are under-funded, not because they couldn't qualify for a commercial loan, but because they don't fit into the traditional ways by which commercial loans are granted or administered.

In his book *A Passion for Success* (an important read for any young entrepreneur), founder of Kyocera and great Japanese entrepreneur Kazuo Inamori said it elegantly:

> *'Too many people think only of their own profit.*
> *But business opportunity seldom knocks*
> *on the door of self-centred people.'*

Mike's mission began that day in upstate New York, and has been buttressed by an amazing team of engineers, valuation experts, data scientists, advisory board and board members, his supportive wife and family, their loyal dog Briggs – and some luck and pretty good market timing.

Like every important journey, it has been incredibly rewarding, with its share of fateful turns and twists. In the beginning they were alone in the field. Only they had the proper software in the cloud. There were a lot of calculators out there – just throwaway solutions – but no one was helping business owners answer *'How much is my business worth?'* accurately.

BizEquity now has over 60 patents and inventions pending, and seven patents already granted for their Intellectual Property (IP).

But it wasn't all plain sailing.

Mike funded operations for the first few years with his own money, on a last in, last out basis every month.

The hardest part was not the bootstrapping, because it taught them a great deal about costs and how far, when things are tightly managed, a dollar can go. They had no choice but to be lean and to focus on the product first.

Service providers had to want to work with them, and be fair with pricing.

Finding the right capital or investment partner is always critical. An investor's goals should line up with yours. If you follow the wrong one, even if they seem terrific and they have approached you, you can end up not proceeding and wasting a lot of time.

Marc Benioff, the founder and CEO of SalesForce, shares a story from the early years at Salesforce.com about travelling for 26 hours to Asia, then driving for another 11 hours, to make a presentation. The night before, he learned that only three people would be at the event, which had been arranged for over 100 attendees. He still made the further 11-hour car journey. Because he went, and fulfilled his commitment, he met a future account that later became responsible for millions of dollars in revenue for his company in the early years.

Mike himself had a false alarm. The fledgling BizEquity seemed to have found a great investor, a multibillion-dollar media and information company. Everything was on course, but the week before the investment was to be approved, a senior executive of the firm (BizEquity's prospective executive sponsor) was brought down by a well-publicized scandal.

Mike recalls clearly that he had read it in a newspaper when he was on a plane for a business trip, and later received a phone call from his point person at the media conglomerate.

In retrospect, it was a great turning point: BizEquity hunkered down, focused on the basics, and accepted that it was not meant to be.

Another bump in the road came after meeting one of the top insurance companies in the world. After a hard nine-month-long sales process, they finally got budget approval for moving forward: a large seven-figure, multi-year enterprise software agreement.

On the day it was to start, their executive sponsor resigned to join a smaller insurance company closer to his home, three states away. A cost-centric finance executive took his place, and the BizEquity project was put on hold. That was rough.

Four weeks after Michael's first child was born, he reluctantly flew to London after a preliminary call with a potential investor who was brought to BizEquity by someone he trusted and respected immensely: best-selling author on entrepreneurship – and co-author of this book – Daniel Priestley.

He almost decided not to leave his new baby and fly 4,000 miles to meet a potential investor about whom he did not know much, in a country he loved but where there were no major clients yet. BizEquity wasn't looking for outside capital, but something told him that he had to go.

He is always grateful that he did. He met not just investment partners, but someone Mike would later call his spiritual business partner and co-founder.

He also met Miles Frost, the founder of the investment group Frost Brooks, a UK boutique private equity firm, whose contacts and relationships have helped BizEquity land major accounts. The capital they provided was critical; it helped take the product global, enable the birth of their award-winning advisor office product line (Advisoroffice.bizequity.com) and add key engineering and development talent to extend the team's market lead. Until then, Mike had been the largest investor.

Like Marc Benioff's story from SalesForce.com's early days, you never know where your journey will take you. The key is to be open-minded and embrace the opportunity regardless of where it is or if it's at a convenient time. Board Member John Loftus likes to always remind Mike that, 'entrepreneurship is a marathon and not a sprint'.

The Good Luck

BizEquity was helped early in its journey in a big way by being able to acquire assets that have enabled it to self-fund the business and limit outside capital requirements in the early years, allowing them to wait to raise capital until four years later.

Through John Loftus, a board member, now investor, and good friend, they heard about an initiative at a billion-dollar bank that had been building a business valuation scoring system to help make better risk-adjusted lending decisions. The bank learned the hard way (which is still standard today for most lenders): asking credit card holders (who were business owners or businesses) for just their credit score, and current income figures was not the best way to go about this. It did not give the whole financial story of a business.

Often, to keep up with their cash flow, their clients would take cash advances out on their cards. Business owners kept their high credit scores and had fairly high current income – but their business values were plummeting. They were essentially taking non-secured debt out on the business at the expense of the company balance sheet.

So the bank thought: if they could figure out what the cardholders' underlying businesses were worth, they could be in a better position to understand credit capacity and risk. A great and forward-looking idea, based on real need to better understand risk.

Unfortunately for their own business, they discovered it too late as the billion-dollar portfolio they had developed through the 80s and 90s had become insurmountable during the credit crunch of 2009.

BizEquity was able to acquire this great asset at a very large discount (with the benefit of the bank already having spent millions of dollars in research and development) and applied it to the product Mike and his team were building.

So in late 2010 the new BizEquity was born.

BizEquity's mission is to democratize the most important knowledge any business owner or their advisor could have.

Today, BizEquity has U.S. headquarters near King of Prussia, Pennsylvania's tech hub, and operational offices in the United Kingdom, India and Singapore.

Company culture

BizEquity has a strong sense of cultural identity as a company. Mike Carter says, 'No matter who they are or what they do; whether they're the CEO, VP, or an associate, everyone on our team needs to do primary work.

'If you're a salesman you have to be able to do your own proposals and presentations; If you're running engineering you also have to be able to code. I think that's what we've done really well. We want to keep that.

'We are a tribe that happens to be a company. I think companies fail when they get properly funded and then hire a whole layer of management that doesn't actually do primary work. We've been very cautious with that.'

Future plans

In the five years it has operated, BizEquity has grown to become the early market leader, having helped 33 million businesses around the world answer *'how much is my business worth?'*.

And it's still growing: it has recently expanded in to the UK, and opened a new Asia-Pacific headquarters in Singapore. BizEquity opened in India in February of 2016 where there are over 43 million businesses and data exists on only 63,000 of them.

'We want to make the most critical financial knowledge available for every business owner and entrepreneur worldwide,' says Michael, 'And we have partnered with over 150 financial institutions and 700 advisors to make that possible.'

BizEquity's Advisor Office service recently launched and is already being used by hundreds of firms. This will enable BizEquity's big data insights and business valuation knowledge to become more widely available to financial and insurance advisors, as well as businesses across the US, the UK and Singapore.

> *Our mission at BizEquity is to value every business in the world and for us to do that it is important that our platform becomes more accessible through financial institutions and advisors across the globe to help the business owners they are already working with know more.*

3

Why Valuation is the Most Important Number You Will Ever Know

By now you will have realized that we are passionate about our mission: to help business owners of all kinds and at all levels to be able to accurately value their businesses at any time. And this kind of knowledge can help businesses avoid all sorts of problems.

One true example of this is the case of a couple in their early sixties, who have a great business, with revenues of over $800,000, that has been trading for over 20 years.

Unfortunately, they can't give it away.

They once dreamed of passing the business on to their children. All three kids have worked for the business at some point, and all three are capable of taking it over – *if* they wanted to. Unfortunately, none of them does.

The business once turned over nearly $2M in revenue. At its peak the business exhibited at trade shows, had a few sales people on the road and spent money on advertising. The last seven years, however, have been more about lifestyle, and things have changed. The family has not been focusing on growing the business. Revenue has dropped each year, and the accounts are not showing huge profits even though the owners are living a relatively good life.

When they tried to sell the business, the declining revenues and negligible profits put off the buyers. No serious offers came in.

None of the nine staff wanted the business either. If they had the money they'd be off doing something else. A management buyout wasn't going to work because there weren't any other managers.

So the decision was finally made to wind down the business and run a few projects from home. At best the business would clear $70k and take up a few days a week.

This kind of depressing exit story is a lot more common than you think.

Just a few hours of planning per year and a tiny amount of money could have changed everything. The couple could have conducted annual valuations of the business; they could have built a list of potential acquirers and planned several exit strategies that would have yielded north of $500k for the exact same business.

This couple could have received several lump sum amounts for their business, plus interest and consulting fees. Instead of working a few days a week for low wages, they could have been travelling, investing, supporting their kids more, or even starting a new and more exciting business.

Had they had a business valuation report each year, they would have identified potential buyers, they would have been able to negotiate effectively, and they would have realized the value of their asset by making better decisions.

It's stories like these that we at BizEquity want to change. We want you to get the most money for your business or your client's business at the most opportune time. We want you to be armed with the information that makes that outcome more achievable.

The cost of inaccurate valuation results

An improperly-valued business can cost you thousands and even millions of dollars; money can either be left on the table when the sale is made, or you can pay far more than a business you are buying is worth.

There's also the unseen cost that creeps up when you're flying blind. Business owners who are armed with relevant information make better decisions, and over time this really adds up. If you were working towards a higher valuation for the last five years, you'd end up with a higher valuation today than if you were only focused on the sales numbers. It's energizing and motivating to see your business value climb year on year.

12 reasons to get your company valued

The main reason you need to have your company properly and accurately valued is to maximize the value you receive from your business. What is measured tends to improve, and valuation is no different. There are several scenarios in which you'll benefit from knowing the real value of your business.

A full exit: This is how the rich get rich. They build a business and sell it for a whopping big capital gain. Could you do this? Maybe. Can you do this without a valuation? No.

A partial exit: This is where someone buys some of the shares in your business, and you can take some money off the table. If there are multiple share sales you'll need a valuation each time.

Investment: When someone puts money into your business to help it grow, they will want to see your business plan, your shareholders' agreement, an investor memorandum and a valuation. If you're growing fast, you might be better off paying an advisor to construct a Discounted Cash Flow to help you maximize the future value of the business.

A restructuring: If you're buying out shareholders, moving jurisdictions, changing your legal entities or acquiring new companies to add to yours, you'll likely need to have an independent valuation completed.

Acquisition or share-swap: If your business is buying a complementary business and exchanging cash or shares in the deal, you should value both businesses to ensure the deal is completed properly.

A separation of partners: The business you and your partner started might have grown, but the relationship you once shared has worn out. This might be the time for one of you to buy the other out. There's no point arguing over valuation – get the report as a starting point and negotiate on the finer details.

A divorce: If you or one of your major shareholders gets divorced, the shares are probably going to be part of the settlement, and you'll need to be armed with a valuation to ensure all your options are open. You don't want the shock of discovering the other side has done their homework and engineered a value you don't agree with.

Creating an employee bonus program: We all love the idea of having a workforce who treat the business like it was their own, but you can't expect them to feel that way if it's not actually the case. An employee incentive scheme can create a high performance culture, especially when employees can see the needle moving on the value of their shares.

Tax planning: Wealth builders plan ahead so they pay the least tax necessary, and a valuation report can lead to additional benefits you might not otherwise claim.

Insurance: Over 70% of all small businesses are underinsured and have no way of recovering lost value in the event of loss that wasn't their fault. If ever you were injured or wrongfully distracted from your business, a historical valuation could be worth real money for you, especially if you have considered this in your insurance choices.

Managing a portfolio of businesses: If you own shares in a number of private businesses, you're typically unaware of the value of your portfolio until they start to sell, but that could be years away. A smarter approach is to value the businesses at regular intervals, and monitor the portfolio over time so you can be a more thoughtful investor/shareholder.

Satisfying your curiosity: Let's be honest: who's not curious about the value of their business? It may be your most valuable asset, so you should know how much it's worth. Business valuation and key performance indicators (KPIs) serve as regular health checks for your business.

The cost of improper valuation

If you do not do get an accurate valuation for your business, you will find yourself at a great disadvantage, especially in the following circumstances:

Caught by surprise: A divorce is a difficult experience on its own, but when a business is involved, decades of hard work are put at risk. When one side does a valuation, and the other side is left clueless, it makes for a nightmare situation. Similar complications can also arise with business partners who fall out, civil lawsuits, and tax audits.

Uninsured: Injuries through negligence are some of those things that people perceive as improbable worst-case scenarios, but they do happen and it can result in you not being able to work for a year. Not only do you lose a year's worth of income, the value of your business would also drop. Are you insured for that? Could you prove it? Wouldn't you like to be able to?

An offer that seems great at the time: You're working away and someone walks in and makes you an offer to buy your business. The money is enough to cover your mortgage *and* pay for a nice new car in full – naturally you'd accept the terms! But what if you later discovered that the true value of your business was much higher and you could have negotiated a boat, a ski chalet and school fees for your kids on top? Now you're kicking yourself!

Equity snatchers: When you're at a low point emotionally, you might agree to things you'd never even consider under normal circumstances. There are people who take advantage of this and solve basic problems for businesses in exchange for large portions of equity (sometimes all of it!). They know you might be feeling your business is worthless and you don't have the time or energy to seek an independent value. If you know the value of your business, you know what you are really giving away if you do a deal. Knowing your value could also give you more robust confidence.

Years of retirement: It's easy to keep turning up and solving day-to-day business problems for years that turn into decades. But if you knew your business was worth enough money for you to retire today, would you choose to spend more years working or would you take your early retirement? Some people would opt to stay, but it's still nice to have the choice. A business often hits its peak value without its owner noticing. At this point they could choose to sell and receive a considerable financial payoff. If they are unaware of the value of their business, time passes, value declines, and any possibility of a big financial pay-out (the one that would've been possible if the owner had known the value of the business in the first place) slips out of reach.

A perfect partnership: Strong foundations are key to making a partnership work, and a measurable goal that gets partners into alignment can be the key to unleashing creativity and drive. Without common goals that can be determined by valuation, the partnership can go lukewarm.

The trillion-dollar dilemma

If a *small* business owner does not know the correct value of their company, they face complications and problems that impede growth, as we have shown. But what happens on a larger scale?

With big businesses, not knowing the company's value becomes a huge and widespread economic problem – one with an international reach.

The USA and Canada have over 27 million businesses, Europe over 20 million, and Australia and New Zealand over two million. Of these 50 million or so businesses, more than half are owned by baby boomers – those born between 1946 and 1964. They control two-thirds of all assets in the international economy. When they want to sell their businesses on, the problem deepens. Anything that challenges them – such as ignorance of business valuation and its consequent problems – challenges the whole economy.

In the next 10 years the Federal Reserve estimates that more than 25 million businesses globally will change hands, 7.7 million within the US alone. This calls for a reality check. Selling a business is not as easy as people think, especially if they have left this to the last possible moment. This is understandable of course – their business is their baby, and the emotional ties are strong.

It might be easier for people to move on if they knew the value of their business, and had a realistic idea of how much money they would receive by selling it. In short – are they going to be able to fund a comfortable retirement?

According to the Business Owner Succession Planning Survey by the Financial Planning Association (FPA) and CNBC, 78% of small business owners plan to sell their businesses to fund their retirement. This would be all well and good, were it not for the fact that fewer than 30% of these have *any* kind of succession plan, even though they have spent their lives building successful businesses. Any financial planner worth their salt will have advised them to prepare for their retirement by sorting out a succession plan, but very few business owners will have followed this sensible advice.

A small business is probably its owner's largest asset, but owners often avoid addressing the matter of how to pass it on – for all sorts of reasons. They feel they do not have the time to spend on preparing it for sale – which involves finding out its accurate value. Or, they don't want to spend the money they think it will cost, or they haven't faced head-on the problem of who they would like to take over their business, or they think it is worth a great deal more than people are prepared to pay for it.

'You can have an owner who insists his business is worth $1 million, but his employees say they wouldn't give him $300,000,' says Martin Kurtz, a certified financial planner and president of The Planning Center. 'It is important to get to a common denominator.'

It's when owners decide to sell, or hire a business broker, investment banker or Mergers and Acquisitions (M&A) advisor or consultant – if they can afford to do so – that the writing is on the wall. Unlike 99% of businesses out there, the Wall Street banks that care for the 1% of businesses are focused on growth and not earnings. This means they focus on Earnings Before Interest, Taxes, Depreciation, and Amortization (EBITDA) or Discounted Cash Flow (DCF).

These have been run to be tax efficient and have little year-end earnings, let alone high growth. This leads business owners to often *understate* their value. To keep it lean they don't add back many of the expenses and related financials into the SDE or Sellers Discretionary Earnings figures.

The result? Disaster.

Entrepreneurs need to know the implications of this strategy, and to know how to find out more information about this.

Valuing a business the day you decide to sell it is like planning for your retirement the day you decide to retire.

It won't work.

Aside from the typical complications in daily operations, a business may also face bigger, game-changing issues at any point in its lifetime. For these situations especially, an accurate business valuation can help keep you protected from financially crippling outcomes.

Overpaying (or leaving money on the table)
If you do not have an accurate idea of the value of your business, you could either sell your business for too little, or

the purchaser could buy it for too much. Whatever happens, someone is not going to be happy.

Divorce

If a divorce can negatively impact a small business, it can certainly do the same for a big one. Divorce settlements can pose bigger risks for a company whose financial and economic activity has an international reach.

Partner Buy-In

Involving a new partner in the company could reveal some improper or unfavourable motivations later on. After the transaction, the partners buying in may not be happy if they find out that they've paid too much. Or the existing members of the business lose motivation because the new partners didn't pay enough for something that could be worth more.

The aim is to have the most appropriate valuation so that everyone involved feels fairly treated.

Partner Buy-out

In order to buy out a leaving partner, a company has to raise money among the remaining partners. Sometimes they have to over-leverage (take on too much debt) to make the required payments, and in the end, the company that remains isn't as strong or valuable than before the buy-out, not because of the partner lost, but because of the debt taken on.

Shareholder Dispute

If the shareholders cannot come to an amicable estimate of what they are owed, or what the business is worth and how much of it they should each have, then it is a minefield. Unfair outcomes and excessive legal fees are just some of the problems that could arise.

Key Man Insurance

This is insurance larger companies take out in case something were to happen to a key person within the company.

Starting and growing a small business demands all of your time and effort, and chances are you haven't thought much about key man insurance: a form of life insurance on one or more key persons in a business (usually the owner). By insuring key persons in your business, you are protecting its integrity, and simultaneously your employees, vendors and most importantly your family.

The valuation of your business will help to determine the amount of coverage needed to sustain it as a going concern under the worst of circumstances.

Business Failure due to Lack of Capital in Time of Need

Every business owner seeks to maximize profits, but many do not realize that profits can sink a business through a growing need for working capital (liquid financial assets). Lack of working capital presents several problems including:

- Inability to pay expenses and obtain discounts
- Creditor indifference
- Pressure to collect payments
- Difficulty in keeping up with competitors

Proactively making arrangements for additional capital before it's needed is a sign of proper management. Having a current business valuation to show your lender indicates a level of sophistication, and can greatly aid in obtaining funds.

Employee Stock Ownership Plan (ESOP)

Business valuations are required at various stages within the life of an ESOP, including:

- When exploring the pertinence of an ESOP for a given business
- For the initial plan to fund the ESOP
- For all annual required valuations for plan trustees
- For valuations to terminate an ESOP

Valuing your business ahead of incurring the expenses to set up, fund and manage an ESOP will help establish the viability and benefits of this tool by gauging the proceeds available to the owners at the time of sale.

Estate/Gift Taxation

After a lifetime of hard work building a business, the thought of losing it all due to inadequate long term estate planning should sufficiently motivate most business owners to take proper courses of action. Sadly, according to numerous surveys, this is not the case.

An estate tax is levied on assets (tax on capital) inherited by the heirs to a deceased person's estate. Consider a 45% estate tax on a $10 million business: without proper planning, the approximate tax burden (after exemptions) would be close to $2.25 million. Needless to say, this type of cash obligation can be devastating to a business and its long-term viability.

Business valuation is the linchpin of estate and gift tax

planning, as a business is most often the largest single asset in the owner's estate.

SBA Loans
(in Britain this is Sale and Purchase Agreement – SPA)
The Small Business Administration loan program in the US is a popular and successful source of credit to those business owners unable to obtain credit elsewhere. All 'change of ownership' loans require a business valuation to support the planned sales price.

When approaching a bank for this type of financing, providing a current business valuation is a sign of sophistication and a source of credibility.

The Six Deadly Sins
Even if you do currently have a correct valuation, you must look at the health of your organization and its staff. Here are Six Deadly Sins to avoid if business owners want to have a clear and current idea of their business' worth, so that they can continue to grow it if they wish. These are the six negative stages of a business under stress, and they can leave owners feeling undervalued and frustrated. Let's talk in the context of valuation.

1. **No Money to Invest:** You have lots of ideas but no money to make them happen. You watch your competitors

getting ahead of you, even though your idea was streets ahead in the first place. Every idea you try to get going needs investment, and you are unable to attract this. Investors just aren't biting.

2. **No Growth:** Your business isn't moving at the speed you want. You know where you want to go with it, you know it will be good for profits and will take your business to the next level, which will make all the difference to further growth, but you don't have the money to take it there, and can't seem to get it either. There is always a stumbling block.

Attracting clients by offering them a truly innovative service –

Chris Roehm, Financial Advisor in Ft. Lauderdale Florida

If a business offers a truly innovative service, clients – both existing and potential – want it. Chris, a financial advisor, carries out estate planning to manage the wealth of clients in South Florida. Part of his offering is to help protect these clients with buy-sell agreements for companies of which they are business partners, and for key person insurance coverage to protect the families of business owners who have most of their net worth tied up in a business.

Historically, the tools he has at his disposal are:

- CRM (customer relationship management) products like Salesforce.com that allow him to document leads or put client contact details in a database
- Estate Planning technology to measure clients' worth (but all estate planning technologies on the market today only measure assets, stocks, bonds, real estate NOT business value)
- Portfolio management technologies to help him to better manage future clients' money and assets.

Like for most financial advisors or insurance agents, Chris' biggest and best clients have been business owners or entrepreneurs. But it has been tough to reach that market. Ten business owners he called over a few months, starting in May 2014, all told him not to call again.

Chris came across BizEquity and wondered:

'If I could answer the business owners' million dollar question of "What is my business worth?" as part of my up-front sales process, I could show these prospects that I am willing to invest in them and deliver something of value they need and maybe have never had the time or money to cover.'

He called back all 10, and told them about this new product and its benefits to their business. He asked them the question again: 'And guess what? Eight allowed me to come in and meet them – and I landed six of them as new clients!'

No Profit: You're making sales but there's no money in the bank and the accountant isn't impressed. The way the business is set up means that money is not going into profits; there may be good reasons for this, but owners and shareholders are not going to feel cheerful. You need to make them happier, and you are stuck about how to do this. The balance sheet is looking thin, and you are worried that this may have negative long-term effects.

3. **No Culture:** You don't have partners or employees who are performing the way you want. Every successful business needs to have its own culture – it needs to know where it came from, what it wants to do and where it wants to go. You realize that you may have chosen the wrong people, or the people who were right for the business at the beginning have not followed your thinking, and so it may be time to separate. You may want to fire them but know that this will be expensive, or you may know people who think the along the right lines, but you can't afford to employ them as things stand. You need to strengthen the culture of the organisation by working with people who get the whole picture and want to make things happen.

4. **No Life:** Your business takes up too much of your time. It's your baby, and you really care about it. You think you need

to give it all your time to make it succeed, and you are resentful when this doesn't make the difference you need: when it begins to affect your family and your leisure time (if you have any). Your business is so stressful that even when you're not in the office you're anxious.

GOOD MORNING...
YOUR BUSINESS
IS WORTH £13M
TODAY

5. **No End in Sight:** You can't see how things will change. You have been slogging away for a long time, and despite some small gains or some larger ones, you are still giving all your time (spare or otherwise) to the business. Your marriage is suffering because your partner complains that you're never there, and is sick and tired of being let down. You can see her problem, but yours is that you can't see how it is going to change.

It doesn't have to be all doom and gloom, however.

We have all heard and been inspired by so many great entrepreneurial stories. These creation stories have inspired millions to follow suit and chase their dreams. In fact, I like to say the athlete of the 21st century is the entrepreneur.

Whether it's Peter Thiel and Elon Musk's story of PayPal in Silicon Valley in the 90s; Richard Branson and the development of one the world's most favorite brands, Virgin in London, in the 70s and 80s; or Rupert Murdoch, who came from Australia to build one of the most dominant media brands in the world over 50 years with News Corp. All these entrepreneurs focused on their own distinctive competencies to develop and grow their 'Enterprise Value'. They leveraged their enterprise value (or their business value) to raise capital to acquire companies, as was the case with PayPal; to form joint ventures to develop brand extensions as Virgin has; or to add world-class talent to their teams like News Corp did. They all knew the power and importance of focusing on their business value in order to grow and receive the capital, talent, or acquisitions needed to win.

The media loves to dwell on stories of millionaires who sold their business, and lay back on the loot. Their start-up story and how they won their first deal makes good copy, and so do the big exit numbers and the names of those who acquired the company. But the journey in between rarely gets the same attention.

In the next chapter we will highlight the four questions every business owner, large or small, needs to answer.

4

How Does a Business Valuation Strengthen a Business?

Knowledge is power. If you know what a business is really worth, and know that that valuation has been completed by an unbiased professional, it becomes a tool that allows you to keep ahead of your potential purchasers and your competitors. It also gives managers and shareholders a way of measuring achievement, profit, loss, and so on – information almost as valuable as the business itself.

The four key questions an owner needs to answer

Any valuation needs to answer four key questions in order to arrive at a business valuation that is accurate, reliable, based on the correct criteria and up-to-date information, and would stand independent assessment by an impartial third party.

1. What is the primary purpose of the valuation? What is at risk?

Business Valuation is the essential process that helps an entrepreneur understand how they are performing. As Warren Buffet has put it, business valuation is the heart of investment and risk management, and without it, you are flying blind. It is the metric that matters most for the exit value of your business; for your lending capacity and credit; and for how much insurance coverage you need as a business or business owner.

With so much dependent on knowing how much your business is worth, the risk is not doing it at all.

2. What is being valued: past, present or future? Equity or enterprise?

All of the above. BizEquity's methodology, in particular, takes into account the past, current and future performance projections, and calculates Enterprise, Equity, Asset, and Liquidation Value figures respectively.

If someone were to get out of a business today, the valuation would be based on the **past and present** of the business (equity). If an investor were to think about investing in the business, they would be buying into **future** growth, and thus the valuation would need to cover potential (enterprise).

For instance, if a small business that had been going for only three months suddenly won a contract with British Airways, the **enterprise** valuation would look bright, but the **equity** valuation would not be very high.

3. What are the different standards that apply to this business valuation?

Business valuation is based on generally-accepted business valuation principles and procedures, which range from basic financial concepts such as the **time value of money** (a dollar today is worth more than a dollar in the future), to complex tools such as the **Black & Scholes option valuation formula**. There is also a concept known as **standard of value**, which refers to the type of value conclusion being generated, and **investment value** or value to a specific or known purchaser, of which strategic value is a variant.

The most common standard of value is **fair market value**, and it's based on a hypothetical buyer and seller, who are under no duress and engage in a full exchange of all information. Fair market value is typically the basis for valuations for tax purposes, whereas business acquisitions are often valued from the perspective of investment value.

The business owner may be interested in one or more of these different standards of value, as they will be associated with varying magnitudes of value.

4. What is the most appropriate method of calculating the value of a business?

Should you use an income, market or cost approach?

The **income approach** is based on what the business is earning.

The **market approach** is based on what other similar companies have sold for in the past. Most buyers will not pay more than what other equally desirable substitutes have sold for and Bizequity has access to literally hundreds of thousands of 'market comps'.

A **cost approach** is based on how much has been put into a business. For example, owners of a construction company who had spent $3million on equipment would not wish to sell it for less than the money they had invested.

Why do you need a valuation?

SME business owners need to know the value of their business when deciding they want to sell it, but it is also necessary when they are making such decisions as those listed below. To better explain, we've used case studies that we feel best represent the points being discussed.

Buying another business to expand

Getting investment for your business

Warren V. 'Pete' Musser, Investor and Venture Capitalist

For over 60 years Warren V. 'Pete' Musser has been investing in small businesses and entrepreneurs. A legendary investor in the United States, he has invested in four multibillion-dollar companies when they were just ideas or with fewer than 20 employees.

These investments have included QVC, the first electronic web- and TV-based shopping channel; Comcast, the world's largest cable company and broadcasting network; Novell, the first billion-dollar networking technology company; and Cambridge Technology Partners, the first publicly-traded IT consulting company.

Pete has looked at over 10,000 companies or start-ups, and has met over 100,000 entrepreneurs.

He has invested in 589 companies, 23 venture capital or private equity funds, and has created over $200billion in shareholders' equity over his career.

He has invested over $12.4 billion dollars personally or in behalf of the funds or investment companies he has started.

He asks one question at the end of every company presentation – even now.

It is simple: *'What do you think the business is worth?'*

He is always astounded that, however successful the entrepreneur is or was, how old he or she is or how much experience he or she has, nine out of ten can't answer the question clearly, or at all.

So what he tells them is: 'Knowing what your business is worth when raising capital or asking for investors could literally be a million-dollar question.'

Passing the business on to family members
When family and business matters collide
Karen and Brian Wagner

The Wagners, who owned a family accounting business, did some excellent estate planning years ago. Karen and Brian, the parents, placed much of the stock in their eldest son's hands, while putting other assets in trust for the remaining children. The parents tried their best to make sure the gifts were roughly equal from a valuation standpoint.

The Great Recession of 2008 changed everything.

The family business is now struggling, and suddenly Jim, the eldest son and CEO, may have a legacy that is worth less than that of the other children.

A valuation of the business will help Karen and Brian determine how much the business is really worth, and can help them decide what estate planning changes may be appropriate. For example, because Jim's share of the legacy (the family business) is suffering, Brian and Karen may decide to change their life insurance designations so that he would receive more than the children not involved in the business.

Breaking up a business and sharing its worth with the business partners

Partners in a profitable technology company decide to go their separate ways

David Gulian, CEO Futura Mobility, Ft. Washington P.A. Technology Entrepreneur and Investor

David and two partners invested in a company called Logistar Solutions, a Systems Applications Product (SAP) software consultancy based in Toronto, Canada. Logistar's speciality is being able to consult and integrate warehousing and logistics technology of SAP for large businesses. They are one of 13,000 SAP consultancies in the US alone, but they are distinguished by their focus.

It only took them five years to become profitable, earning more than $14,000,000. The partners then decided it was time to sell, as each had different needs. So, they went to an IT services-centric boutique investment bank who told David and his co-founders that their business was worth six times earnings and no more – roughly $10.8million to $12million.

Although this figure seemed to be good for all involved, the partners were unconvinced. Before signing on with the investment bank, David did some research. He found BizEquity.com online, put in the figures of the business, and paid $365. The BizEquity report he received listed four business valuation figures (Asset, Equity, Enterprise and Liquidation), and cites a value of between $18.4million and $22.7million.

The BizEquity algorithm and systems recognized the business was run to be tax-efficient, and automatically reapplied some of the officer compensation into the earnings figure to compute a technical angle called Seller's Discretionary Earnings (or 'SDE figures'). While the valuation multiples might have been similar to what the previous investment banker mentioned, the actual earnings figures were different because some of the owners' pay should have been calculated as profit. The result? A $7million change in value. Another result? The partners of Logistar used that report to interview other investment bankers who subscribe to a similar philosophy.

In June 2014, a leading accounting and technology consulting company – the fourth largest in the world – bought Logistar for more than $22million.

The BizEquity engine was within 2% of the purchase price!

A $365 spend has helped generate $7.2million dollars in the deal!

Bringing in new partners or investors

It's an exciting time when a business brings in a new partner or investor – or at least, it *should* be. To make sure it is, you'll need to make sure that your prospective partners and investors know everything they need to know about your business: what it has achieved, what projects it has lined up, what campaigns it has run, and especially what it's worth. Providing prospective partners and investors an accurate, up-to-date valuation of your business helps reassure them so that they feel secure in where their money is going.

Knowing this, a software development entrepreneur whose business was on the brink of an international expansion invested in receiving the best and most efficient business valuation he could afford. When he finally found the right partners to help fund and enact the next stage of his business plans, the expansion went smoothly – no unexpected road bumps or conflicts, which meant no delays. The business valuation not only helped the entrepreneur to attract the right partners, it helped the process go so smoothly it could barely even be called a negotiation!

The partners liked what they saw, and never once felt short-changed by the partnership agreements. What a great way to start a new phase of a thriving business!

Resolving commercial disputes
You will need a business valuation if you are challenged in court, when a valuation issue rises to the level of litigation.

A family-owned business in the USA recently had their case go all the way to their state's supreme court because the family disagreed over the correct valuation for buying out a sibling. Having a recent and accurate business valuation would certainly help to facilitate such tedious situations much more efficiently.

Divorce or estate planning matters

There are many different reasons why people need to sell a business. Often, business partners want to go their separate ways for professional reasons. However, sometimes personal and family life comes into play: couples divorce, or they decide to retire and their family doesn't want to be involved with the business. Whatever the situation, the business – probably their biggest asset – needs to be accurately valued by a disinterested third party, so that everyone knows the price is fair.

Wanda and Pete were proud owners of a simple small-town petrol station that had provided most of their family's income for 22 years.

However, they decided to divorce, and so far, negotiations had taken two years, and there was one last thing left to settle: the value of their largest asset, the business that had faced tough times. And when Wanda asked what the business was worth, she was told: 'Nothing.'

Not a promising answer.

Pete told her that his accountant said a valuation would cost at least $5,000, and would take another two months.

Concerned for her livelihood, Wanda contacted the accountant who confirmed that, in his opinion, 'the business isn't worth much, and my fee is expensive. Business valuation is an art form and takes time and effort.'

Refusing to be fobbed off, she scoured the internet and found BizEquity. Following the online platform's simple step-by-step process, Wanda put in the numbers from the last tax return. In seconds, she got a 29-page report on the business.

It told her that the business was worth $447,112 – a far cry from 'nothing'!

She called BizEquity to thank them, before sharing the information with her husband and the accountant.

Seeing an effective product and a great opportunity, the accountant called BizEquity and asked if his company could use the service, and resell the end result for $5,000! Through this case alone, BizEquity proved that it can be a valuable asset for both average consumers, and other businesses and service providers alike!

Getting a high-value exit

According to a recent CNBC Study, over 10 million businesses will change hands over the next 10 years in the U.S. alone. 78% of business owners think they are going to fund their retirement 80-100% by exiting and selling their business, yet few know the true value of their biggest asset: the business itself. Some smart financial planners and advisors are starting to use business valuation as a value added service to prospect and care for their clients, and help them ensure that they can attain the best value exit possible.

One such financial planner is Chris Rhoem, a partner at Freedom Business Advisors. Freedom Business Advisors are dedicated to helping South Florida business owners through their financial, estate (and yes, retirement and exit) plans. Chris has long recognized that most business owners need better financial protection, so that they do not get shortchanged in the event of a business sale or exit. However, many business owners were hesitant to get their businesses valuated because of the time and costs they thought were involved.

'At Freedom Business Advisors, we offer owners a 360-degree view of their business and personal financial situation, and

BizEquity helps me educate my clients exactly where they stand today, so we can properly plan for their futures,' says Chris. 'BizEquity is an essential part of my planning approach to family or closely-held business owners. It helps me create better plans to protect, grow, and transfer the business interests that my clients own.'

By valuing their clients' businesses using BizEquity, Chris has helped business owners stay aware of how much their businesses are worth, and by doing so, they are more assured that when the time comes, they can exit a business in the most financially rewarding way.

Dealing with tax compliance or tax audits

The value of a business is also important in supporting many decisions about the business strategy and development.

A good valuation must not only have a clear explanation of the value of the business, it must also show the evidence to support the result.

Getting the right people motivated (including you!)

Knowing exactly what your business is worth can greatly impact you and your team, while working on your business with inaccurate or unfounded business valuations can have you running around in circles. That's because just like any data relevant to your business, a business valuation can tell you if you need to work harder and refocus your efforts, or, even better, if you're doing the right thing and actually headed in the right direction.

A clothing retail business with a small team was doing everything double-time, double effort. Its owner had been waiting to open a few more branches around the city, and apply for funding from angel investors. However, the business valuation they received told them that the business was not ready, and that it would take at least another two years of consistent operation before it would be.

After some time, the team began to feel demotivated – for all their hard work and hustling, they were still nowhere closer to their goals. Sharing in their frustration, the owner sought a new business valuation through BizEquity. It turns out they've been ready and prime for investment for months! This great news definitely encouraged the team, who eagerly moved on to the next phase of the business.

By having an accurate business valuation completed for your company, you're giving yourself and your team a better and more complete picture. It's great that this clothing retail business were quick to take action, but even then, they could have certainly saved themselves the time, energy and frustration.

Determining capital gains tax liability

A business owner had, for years, used and enforced a book value approach to buying out family members. The family had come to an amicable decision about the value of the company among themselves.

Unfortunately the Revenue Service decided later on that they had valued it too cheaply, it was too large a business, and they owed a large penalty to the Government.

The Revenue ignored the owners' valuation, and instead used one that was higher and earnings-based. In addition to assessing millions more in estate taxes, the revenue also demanded a multimillion-dollar penalty.

Anyone who inherits a family business can encounter this problem especially after the person who started it dies. Those who become involved subsequently, and the business itself, will be put under enormous pressure. If the business is of substantial size, it will attract the attention of the Revenue, who will want to investigate, and, if it decides that taxes are owed, they will have to be paid.

If they had had a realistic valuation of the business, the owners could have had a strong case with which to contest the Revenue valuation. An independent valuation methodology, put in place from the time they decided to split the business up, would have allowed them to argue their case – and very likely win it.

Succession Planning

You may have a key person who wants to share in the success of your business. Even though he or she will not be a successor-owner, you still want to provide the right financial incentives to keep them. Profit, sales and other annual measures may not truly reflect the growth of the business, and may not encourage the long-range thinking you want from that key employee.

This was exactly the case when a profitable and growing real estate development company approached Jenny as a key stakeholder and strategist. Jenny was a highly sought-after expert in diversifying real estate companies' portfolios, so the company needed to make sure that they were as attractive as possible in Jenny's eyes. To be able to offer her the right compensation for her services, they first needed to get an accurate business valuation. This helped them know what they could offer her at the current stage of the business, and what they can offer her later on, after considering the additional profits her expertise can bring in.

Obtaining a current business valuation gives you a baseline value to use in deferred compensation arrangements, such as phantom stock and stock appreciation rights (SAR) plans. Unless you know where you're starting from, you can't measure growth – and you certainly can't expect a key person in your industry to buy into your company's vision either.

Getting rid of the wrong people

Just as business valuations are great for establishing who and what are in line with your business, they're also useful for finding out who and what are all wrong and incompatible. An accurate business valuation provides you, your team and your stakeholders the bigger picture: what your business is worth today, how far it's come, and how much more it can expand. When you have this information, you can better plan what it will take to grow, and find out who just won't make the cut.

A current business valuation helped a catering company move forward with only the best team members and stakeholders who were aligned with the owner's vision. Upon receiving the valuation, Richard, the owner, sat down with his two partners Henry and Liz, and updated their five-year business plan. Unfortunately, Henry did not share the enthusiasm that Richard and Liz had for the growth and direction of the company. Furthermore, they learned that a few members of their team were just not the right fit for the company's future plans.

It was beneficial to the company and to Henry that these incompatibilities were identified and dealt with in time, before the company dove into their plan for the next five years. It could have had such a negative impact on the operations if these surfaced in the middle of trying to put the plans into action.

Protecting The Key Person

It may be easy to overlook the impact a business' value can have on its access to the select suppliers, but in fact, a current valuation may very well determine your choice of suppliers – and consequently what the quality of your final product will be. How much your business is worth can give your suppliers an indication of your financial resources and room for growth. If they find both the present and the future of your business reassuring and appealing, your suppliers will be happy (or even eager) to do business with you, giving you more leverage during negotiations.

An authorized company provider and distributor of Apple hardware and software is more likely to offer a better discount or a more favourable package deal to an independent magazine publisher who may be more low-key in publicity and popularity, but is more consistent and holds more potential for growth financially than to an older, more established publisher who has extensive media and publicity campaigns, but whose business valuation seems riskily overreaching. The computer distributor may choose to service both companies anyway, but they will likely be more flexible and accommodating of negotiations with a company with more certainty.

Getting a successful growth acquisition

After a certain point, your business will seem to just take on a life of its own, and will run like a well-oiled machine (most days of the year). Growth acquisitions will not only become more appealing, they will become more feasible, too. When you think of expanding, you may no longer feel limited to just growing what you have; it could also mean buying new businesses to diversify your portfolio and entrepreneurial activity. But that'll only happen if you can convince existing owners to entrust the product of their own hard work to you.

James built his bottling and packaging company from the ground up, and it has grown to be one of the leading service providers in the country. He feels secure in the direction that his logistics company is headed, and would now like to dip his toes into the wine industry. He's always liked the idea of owning a vineyard and growing a small independent winery, and was confident this passion project could turn into his next big entrepreneurial adventure. And he couldn't deny that his experience in bottling and packaging would greatly complement the wine business, too. He's had his eye on one particular winery for some time, and because he knew that the owners were eager to sell and retire, he thought he would be the proud owner of this winery before the year was over.

He was wrong.

The owners were not so easily convinced to sell to James, and the negotiations went on for much longer than he expected. Not surprisingly, they were sceptical about just how well James could take care of their business, because the valuation he presented for his business was quite underwhelming compared to all the hype around it. The sale did eventually go through, but not until James convinced the winery owners that his new business valuation from BizEquity was more accurate and reliable. But imagine how much time and stress James could've saved himself – and the winery's previous owners – if only the business valuation was good from the beginning!

As a businessperson yourself, you surely understand a company owner's need to see a sound and accurate business valuation from someone who could potentially buy the product of his or her labour. When the roles are reversed, and you are in a position to acquire for growth, remember that you would want to sell to someone whose business-savvy track record is quantifiable.

5

How is a Business Valued?

For you to understand how BizEquity provides businesses around the world with the best and most accurate business valuation, you need to know the terms that will be used whenever the value of your business is discussed. This will also help you be able to jump into negotiations quickly, so that at every step of the way, you're clear on what different parties are saying about your company.

This chapter may get a bit technical, but it will be a vital resource for you, and you can refer to it when you encounter terms or processes that you may find unfamiliar as you go through your own business valuation process.

There are many factors that affect how a business is valued, and there is no doubt that you will need a professional to work out a value for you. This is where BizEquity comes in and you can use the tool it has developed to do this with minimal interference to your and your business' activity.

By asking the business owner for three years' worth of figures, most of which can be obtained from the most recent set of Annual Accounts, the BizEquity system quickly analyses:

Revenue generation
- What revenue trends have occurred in the past, and what can be expected in the future?
- How does the business attract and retain customers?
- How loyal are its customers?
- What resources and systems are in place to support on-going sales?

Business profitability
- What has the profitability been in the past, and what can be expected in the future?
- What investments and initiatives to increase profit margins have been implemented?

Stability

- Does the business face significant changes in its external environment, such as the development of new technology, or changes in market demand and regulation?

- What uncertainty does the business face, and how will this affect cash flow?

- What competition exists within the industry, and will impact the future cash flow of the business and its stability?

Competitive advantage

- Does the business have a well-defined and leveraged competitive advantage?

- To what degree does this competitive advantage generate superior earnings?

- How does the competitive advantage lead to an offering that is better than its competitors?

Industry lifecycle

- Is the industry in a natural decline, or does it have a growing demand?

- Will technology change the industry lifecycle in the near future?

- Will changes in the industry lifecycle impact future earnings?

Reliance on owner-operator

- Does the business rely on its owner and/or key staff?
- How will the earnings of the business be affected by the owner leaving the business?
- What systems and procedures are in place to support and replace the owner and the key staff?

Different Types of Valuation

In understanding and interpreting the value of a business, it is important to recognize that there are many different types and levels of value. The most common scenario involves the estimation of 'fair market value on a going concern basis' for the entire company, e.g. a 100% interest in the subject equity or assets/enterprise.

Fair Market Value

The *International Glossary of Business Valuation Terms* defines a fair market value as:

> [t]he price, expressed in terms of cash equivalents, at which property would change hands between a hypothetical willing and able buyer, and a hypothetical willing and able seller, acting at arm's length in an open and unrestricted market, when neither is under compulsion to buy or sell and when both have reasonable knowledge of the relevant facts.

In other words, fair market value is the estimated price at which a fully-informed buyer and a fully-informed seller are free and willing to conduct the sale or transaction.

Going Concern
An on-going operating business enterprise.

Liquidation Value
The net amount that would be realized if the business is terminated and the assets are sold piecemeal. Liquidation can be either 'orderly' or 'forced'.

When valuing the entire company (100% control interest), it is necessary to distinguish between the value of 'assets' (asset deal) and the value of 'equity' (stock deal). In practice, owner-operated businesses are either sold on an 'asset sale basis' or on an 'equity sale basis', with the purchase agreement reflecting the unique aspects of each scenario.

A variety of factors will determine the chosen mode of sale, with buyer and seller negotiating price and an array of other 'terms and conditions' including the type of sale.

Most small private firms are sold as asset sales, while the majority of middle-market transactions involve the sale of equity.

The 'asset sale' value will always differ from the 'equity sale' value due to the specific group of assets and liabilities that are included or excluded in each format.

In determining which estimations of value are of most relevance to the business owner, the reason behind the valuation will typically address this question. Business brokers hired to assist buyers and owners often value businesses under the 'asset sale' scenario through multiples of discretionary earnings, while valuations for divorce or estate taxes will be based primarily on the 'equity sale' scenario.

The general differences between the asset and equity transaction structure are:

Asset Sale (Asset Value)
Includes *only* inventory/supplies, fixed assets and all intangible assets. Excludes all liquid financial assets and all liabilities. Buyer operates from newly-formed legal entity.

Equity Sale (Equity Value)
Includes the assets listed above *plus* liquid financial assets *less* all liabilities (ST/LT).

Involves the full transfer of the legal entity including all account balances and current tax attributes.

Naturally, the 'value' associated with these two distinct transactions can be substantially different. In practical terms:

Asset Sale

The seller keeps the cash and receivables, but delivers the business free and clear of all debt.

Equity Sale

The buyer is acquiring ALL the assets and liabilities, on and off the balance sheet.

In the real world, there are many variations on these basic structures, such as an asset sale might include accounts receivable or an equity sale might exclude long-term debt etc. The values provided in this report are stated in terms of the baseline case as defined above. They are both 'fair market value on a going concern basis' estimates, but one reflects the asset sale and one reflects the equity sale.

Enterprise Value

In middle-market transactions, it is also helpful to distinguish between 'equity value' and 'enterprise value'. Enterprise value is a reflection of the firm's value as a functioning entity and it is helpful in that it facilitates the comparison of companies with varying levels of debt.

Which Business Value conclusion is most important?

The answer to this question depends chiefly on the purpose for the valuation engagement. If you are negotiating the sale or purchase of a business by way of an asset sale, then it is the asset value that is most relevant. Meanwhile, the equity value is most important if you are filing an estate or gift tax return. When evaluating middle-market companies for M&A purposes, both equity and enterprise value will be useful. If your business is rapidly deteriorating and you are contemplating reorganization, then liquidation value may be of most relevance.

Approaches to Valuation

BizEquity's focus is to try to provide a proprietary and real-world-oriented valuation approach for small, midsize and emerging businesses. In doing so, we include methods from the following valuation approaches utilized by the industry:

Market Approach

This involves an analysis of the recent sales of comparable businesses. In a way, this is similar to how residential real estate is valued, that is, the firm is valued by way of 'market comps'. This implies that the firm is valued based on looking at comparable real time transactions in that particular industry, company size and geography. If you are a restaurant owner in California selling your business, we will leverage data on all the restaurants sold in California to come up with your valuation.

Income Approach

The income approach methods seek to transform measures of profits or cash flow into estimates of value by way of multiples, capitalization rates and discount rates.

Rules of Thumb

These are simple but often powerful valuation methods regularly used by market participants. Some business types are bought and sold almost exclusively by way of these industry-specific rules of thumb.

Asset Sale Value

This common transaction-oriented fair market value conclusion includes the firm's inventory, furniture, fixtures and equipment and all intangible assets ranging from customer base to goodwill.

Enterprise Value

This fair market value estimate is equal to the 'total value of the firm' or the value of the firm's equity plus its long-term debt, e.g. it reflects the value of the entire capital structure (equity holders and debt holders) or 'enterprise'.

Liquidation Value

The liquidation value conclusion is based on the key assumption of insolvency and the immediate sale of all assets (on or off the balance sheet) at or near fire sale level, coupled with the nearly simultaneous retirement of all liabilities. This figure does not include accounts receivable.

The BizEquity valuation is based on information provided by the business under the following headings:

Income	Assets	Liabilities
Turnover	Intangible Assets	Trade Creditors
Profit Before Taxation	Tangible Assets	Other Short-Term Liabilities
	Investments	
Officer Compensation	Stocks	Bank Loans
Interest Expense	Trade Debtors	Other Long-Term Liabilities
Non-Cash Expenses	Cash	Provision for Liabilities
One-Time Expenses	Other Current Assets	
One-Time Revenues		

Key Performance Indicators

We calculate a variety of Key Performance Indicators (KPIs) for our review and comparison to industry benchmarks. In terms of valuation outcomes for your firm, key factors include size, profitability and growth. Here are the main KPIs your BizEquity report will give you:

Return on Equity (RoE) over time

What does it mean?

This is the amount of net income generated as a percentage of shareholder's equity. RoE measures a company's profitability by depicting how much profit a company generates with the money shareholders have. It compares profitability to the equity value of a company, and is also an indication of the strength of the business model.

Why should it matter?

ROE is a universal and very useful measure to compare a company's profitability to that of its peers in the same industry. High growth companies tend to have a high ROE.

For example:

If an e-commerce company has an ROE of 0.48, this means it generated 48 cents in net income for every £1 the shareholder had invested.

Receivables (Conversion) Over Time

What does it mean?

The time period shows the number of days it takes a company to collect its account receivables. Increases over time could signal difficulty in collecting from customers.

Why should it matter?

A shorter time period indicates that a company relies mainly on cash, or is efficient in imparting credit and collecting its debts. On the other hand, a longer time period could mean some inefficiency in collecting the account receivables, and requires a review of the current credit and collections policies of the company. The quicker receivables are collected, the sooner cash is available to meet other business needs, thereby reducing the need to borrow funds.

For example:

If a lumber wholesaler has a receivables conversion of 24 days, it means it takes 24 days on average to collect its account receivables. If the firm's credit terms are 'net 30 days', this would be considered a positive result.

Inventory Turnover Over Time

What does it mean?

Inventory Turnover Over Time refers to how long it takes to sell inventory on hand. This activity or turnover ratio addresses how efficiently goods are sold, by calculating how many times a company's inventory is sold and replaced in a given time period.

Why should it matter?

A lower ratio could mean poor sales and excessive inventory, possibly due to pricing policies. A higher ratio may indicate a too-narrow selection of product, and possibly lost sales and excessive inventory that could be due to pricing policies. Companies selling perishable goods, for example, have a very high inventory turnover. Keeping inventory balances to a minimum will reduce costs but may reduce sales volume.

For example:

If a soda manufacturer had an inventory turnover of 5.7, this means it sold all of its average inventory 5.7 times each year.

Fixed Assets Turnover Over Time

What does it mean?

This activity ratio refers to how productive a company's assets are. It shows the company's ability to generate net sales from their investments in fixed assets.

Why should it matter?

A higher ratio shows productive fixed asset investment. This ratio is more vital and useful to the manufacturing industry.

For example:

If a manufacturing company had a fixed asset turnover of 3.8, this means the company generated sales worth £3.80 for every £1 of investment in fixed assets.

Debt-to-Equity Over Time

What does it mean?

Debt-to-Equity Over Time shows the extent of the debt load in comparison to a company's equity value.

This solvency ratio is a function of the firm's capital structure (wherein all assets must be financed by either debt or equity), and provides a measure of the company's financial leverage. It often takes into account the total liabilities of the company, while some versions include only long-term debt. It indicates the proportion of equity (owner investments and retained profits) and liabilities the company is using to finance its asset base.

Why should it matter?

A higher ratio generally means that the company has been aggressive to finance its growth with debt, and the creditors are assuming a higher risk. On the other hand, a lower ratio generally indicates that the company is safer (i.e. better equipped to withstand an economic downturn) due to lower mandatory principal and interest payments, but it may also suggest an overly cautious ownership. Capital-intensive industries tend to have a higher debt-to-equity ratio than others.

For example:

A machinery manufacturer has a ratio of 2.8. This means that for every £1 owned by the shareholders the company owes £2.80 to its creditors.

Interest Coverage Over Time

What does it mean?

Also referred to as 'times interest earned', this shows how much cushion a company has in paying its interest expenses. This solvency ratio is equal to Earnings Before Interest and Taxes (EBIT) divided by interest expense, and it is used to determine the ease by which a company can pay interest on outstanding debt obligations.

Why should it matter?

A lower ratio may cast doubt on the company's ability to meet on-going principal and interest burdens. But the higher the ratio, the easier it is for the firm to repay its current debt and take on additional debt if necessary. Bankers, creditors and even investors often calculate and analyse this ratio to gauge the firm's solvency position. Similar to most ratios, averages will differ by industry.

For example:

If a software company has an interest coverage ratio over two times, this suggests that it has the ability to meet its interest payments two times over, and may qualify for additional debt.

Cash-to-Debt Over Time

What does it mean?

This solvency ratio shows the ability of a company to pay off existing debts, and compares a company's operating cash balance to its total debt. This ratio provides an indication of the company's ability to cover total debt (both short-term and long-term) with its operating cash holdings.

Why should it matter?

A higher percentage ratio indicates that the company is better equipped to carry and service its total debt. It may also indicate excess cash or excess net working capital, which could be returned to the shareholders or invested into new equipment or other avenues for expansion. A low ratio could signal future difficulties in servicing debt, or even meeting payroll or vendor obligations.

For example:

If a furniture store has a ratio of 74% this means that for every £1 of debt, it has 74 cents in liquid holdings, which could be used to service this debt.

Income-to-Revenue Over Time

What does it mean?

This pre-tax profitability ratio known as 'return on sales' indicates the relative profit margin of the company for each dollar of sales. A rising percentage will often lead to a higher valuation.

Why should it matter?

Similar to the return on equity ratio, a higher percentage ratio indicates a higher rate of relative profitability. However, unlike the return on equity ratio, this measure is pre-tax in nature and is not affected by the actual tax burden. Higher gross profits and lower operating expenses coupled with higher revenues will bolster this important metric, which can be compared both over time and against the industry peer group.

For example:

If a convenience store has a percentage ratio of 17%, this means that for every £1 of revenue it has a pre-tax income of 17 cents.

Cash Flow-to-Revenue Over Time

What does it mean?

This multipurpose ratio is an indicator of the firm's ability to convert sales revenue into spendable cash for the ownership. Often times this is a key measure when analysing a company's ability to grow without the assistance of capital.

Why should it matter?

As with the income-to-revenue over time, a rising percentage in cash flow-to-revenue over time will often lead to a higher valuation. A higher percentage ratio indicates the company is able to turn a higher amount of revenues into cash flow.

For example:

If a winery has a percentage ratio of 11%, it means for every £1 of revenue it is generating around 11 cents in discretionary cash flow.

Receivables-to-Income Over Time

What does it mean?

This measure provides an indication of the amount of credit being granted to the customer base, relative to ongoing profits.

Why should it matter?

If the receivables are greater than pre-tax profit, it becomes more crucial to establish and maintain an effective and efficient credit, billing and collections process.

For example:

A company with £100K in receivables and £100K in pre-tax profit must collect all receivables to maintain the firm's profit margin.

Inventory-to-Income Over Time

What does it mean?

This ratio illustrates the relative importance of inventory holdings (typically carried at lower of cost or market) to company profitability.

Why should it matter?

For retail and manufacturing firms in particular, inventory is one of the factors that you can control to improve your small business profitability. The way that inventory is sourced and managed can impact the different profit levels of your income statement. Ignorance of how to use inventory to your advantage prevents you from maximizing operational efficiency.

For example:

Over time, the goal of a sizable retail clothing chain might be to decrease this ratio by generating higher pre-tax profit with lower average inventory holdings.

Fixed Assets-to-Income Over Time

What does it mean?

This ratio provides insight into the firm's profitability relative to its stock of fixed assets (furniture, fixtures and equipment/vehicles).

Why should it matter?

All other things equal, the firm seeks higher pre-tax profits for each dollar invested into fixed assets. As this ratio declines, the company generates higher profits per dollar of capital expenditures.

For example:

An app development company with a ratio greater than one likely has more money invested into its capital assets than profits have been generated. This and other ratios should be reviewed 'over time' and against industry norms.

Total Debt-to-Income Over Time

What does it mean?

This measure shows the relationship between total company obligations at any point in time (short- and long-term debt) and ongoing profit performance.

Why should it matter?

Firms with high debts relative to pre-tax profits are often riskier than those with lower total debts. At the same time, some companies rely on the use of debt to grow and enhance profit margins, such as when the return on investment of borrowed funds is greater than the cost of borrowing. From a valuation perspective, firms with lower debts and higher pre-tax profits will be worth more than those with higher debts and lower profits (all other things being equal).

For example:

A publishing company with total debts of £100K and total pre-tax profits of £50K would take two years to pay off debts out of ongoing profits.

Exponential Business Value

Businesses of all types and sizes get business valuations because they're interested in discovering what their most valuable asset is worth. Taking this first step is critical, but it's only the first of many. The business value, the next step is to proactively manage it, and this involves monitoring and optimizing the value of your company.

Our goal is to help entrepreneurs climb the valuation mountain illustrated above, to the highest level possible by internalizing certain key valuation and operational concepts associated with discovering, monitoring and optimizing business value.

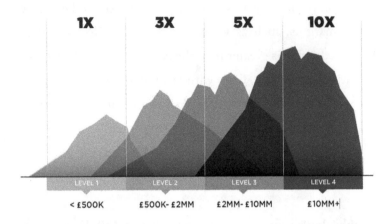

1X	3X	5X	10X
LEVEL 1	LEVEL 2	LEVEL 3	LEVEL 4
< £500K	£500K- £2MM	£2MM- £10MM	£10MM+

Every business will go through stages of development and, hopefully, growth, and we want to be a driver of this process. Once the basics of business valuation are understood, the path towards enhancing value will become clearer and more real in the eyes of the owner.

One central theme that is as simple as it is important concerns the so-called 'size effect' or 'size premium'. It's an empirical fact that companies with higher revenues and earnings are worth more than their smaller counterparts. Achieving exponential value growth is made possible by the dual impact of higher earnings. Among other things, this means that higher earnings will directly increase value at any multiple – *and* higher earnings will alone lead to a higher valuation multiple.

6

The Next Steps to Growing Your Business and Increasing its Value

We at BizEquity believe that the future of lending will see transparency, big data insights, and perhaps the emergence of a new credit-like score for business owners and their businesses. We believe the new score will be BizEquity's business valuation score.

When you reward a business owner for the business value they have built, you cement trust and build that transparency engine by layering in a new system for the business owner to better understand themselves and their business, and so perform better on all fronts.

The future of lending for businesses will be based on transparent business value.

Get your team thinking about valuation

Every manager in a company should be aware of its value. This knowledge will help motivate them to do their job as well as they can, and will give them a realistic idea of how they can contribute to take the company forward. The team should be encouraged to bear an accurate valuation in mind, especially when making important decisions about the company's future development.

Develop assets and keep track of them

A company's assets are not always easily quantifiable. They can be knowledge, products, people, goodwill, plant and equipment, buildings…

This changes throughout the life of a company, and can add to or subtract from a company's value. All employees should be aware of the value of the company at each stage, and make it their business to keep track of assets and their contribution to the value of a company. This requires a valuation that adjusts as factors change.

Measure and document regularly

A company valuation needs to be up-to-date. Assets, problems, clients, increased revenue and so on should regularly be measured and documented, so that anyone who needs to know the value in order to plan for the future can have access to them, and know that the figures are accurate.

Position yourself as valuable

Knowing the value of your business makes you more confident when it's time to negotiate for the best loan options with your bank. This may sound simple, but in truth the impact of this could be significant. You can carry out loan applications and negotiations as an active partner with your bank, reassured by the fact that you and your bank are making decisions based on the same figures, the same report, and therefore standing on the same ground as equals. By having an accurate business valuation that's been carried out well, you open the floor to a more productive and effective dialogue with any party involved.

Business Lending Today

Since the last great recession of 2008, businesses have decided to look elsewhere for growth capital, or simple commercial lines of credit or personal loans. They have embraced alternative lending platforms online that give more credence to other data or risk factors, in an automated and lightning-fast way. The technology term for these new data insights is Big Data.

Big Data is really small, purposed data insights on a particular sequence of questions or on a particular insight.

Some online lending leaders like Steve Allocca, General Manager of PayPal Credit, and Sean Rowles, Chief Risk Officer of PayPal, view this as an opportunity to go a step further still, and provide a new transparency layer to their customers and prospects. Their vision is very powerful: Steve and Sean believe that that the future of lending will be based on trust. Steve's goal is for business owners to say to PayPal one day, 'I trust you, you know me, and you are on my side.'

Clearly this is something business owners have never felt from lenders. It would change everything.

But how do you rebuild that trust in the lending process for business owners? You re-imagine it as a lender. You demand it as a business owner. You provide business owners with a new level of transparency, like PayPal is doing. You make lending instantaneous, happening in real time. You factor in a multitude of so-called Big Data Insights to reward businesses and their owners properly by extending credit based on new machine-learned insights from their actual business.

And this is where BizEquity can make your life a whole lot easier. If you get a valuation the traditional way, you'll spend thousands of dollars, and it will take several weeks. Not good news for busy business owners. You'll be distracted from your core business, and the information you receive may be neither useful nor accurate, because most valuations rely upon very limited data.

By using BizEquity.com you'll get your valuation in under an hour – often in as little as 10-20 minutes. It'll cost a few hundred dollars rather than a few thousand. It will draw upon millions of data-points, so you will end up with an accurate report you can start to work with.

BizEquity's team has many decades of business experience relating to starting, growing, funding and exiting businesses. We use the brightest data scientists who do nothing but figure out ways to find and use as much business valuation data as possible. On top of that, we have a team of the best business schools' brightest minds who lecture on best practice for business valuation.

This is why BizEquity.com is now the most trusted provider of business valuations in the world. We have valued over 30 million businesses, and raised millions of dollars in investment ourselves to make us the very best at business valuation in every corner of the business landscape. Along the way, a trillion-dollar consumer credit industry has been built, as well as a $50-billion-dollar credit scoring industry to support the lenders.

But the small business owner has been left out in the cold.

The Future of Lending

Today, Business owners are treated no differently than consumers when looking to get a loan. The first two questions they are asked are the same:

What is your credit score?
What is your current income?

But most, if not all, successful entrepreneurs don't worry about lining their pockets with short-term current income. They invest in what they're building, so that the enterprise value of the business grows.

So think about it: the two questions that the consumer-lending machine is based on have nothing to do really with the enterprise value of the business. The 'Enterprise Value' of the business, as we have established, are the two most important words for every entrepreneur to discover, monitor and optimize. So wouldn't you think the commercial and business lending markets would be based – at least in part – on understanding and lending to that value, that metric, or that score?

We believe this will happen in the not-too-distant future. Why? Because it will have to. Online lenders are getting smarter every day by asking myriad Big Data analytic questions that show that they can base their risk and credit decisions on other factors. This has helped them grow at a rate of a 5-to-1 ratio against the growth rate of traditional banks and offline lenders.

What if business credit and commercial loans were based on something that all businesses could measure, and manage and strive to grow? What if small business loans were neither consumer-oriented nor based on requirements that hinder their ability to be viewed properly?

When The Fair Credit and Reporting Act of 1970 was established in the United States, it ushered in a period of unprecedented lending capacity and growth for consumer credit. We at BizEquity believe a similar measure is needed to help usher in a boom in lending to the 99% of businesses which are in fact small businesses that need to be judged and measured more fairly.

The Fair Credit and Reporting Act called for personal lenders (such as credit card companies) to treat consumers better through more accurate and representative measures of credit and risk, by establishing the credit score as the common *lingua franca*.

It is our belief that by 2020, the business valuation score will do to business lending what the credit score helped to do to the consumer lending market, making it more available and transparent for entrepreneurs. And we believe BizEquity will be the FICO for businesses around the world.

We believe that if the existing banking infrastructure around the world wants to compete more effectively with offline lenders, they will help to promote this new initiative so that there are new common ways to lend transparently more effectively.

The 2012 presidential election in the United States may have foreshadowed something very important, but perhaps the words were misplaced. Rather than the problem, it's *opportunity* for the economy that stands with the 99% and not the 1%. The 99% are the small businesses globally that need a more transparent and fairer measure by which to be lent to and grow.

Get Started with BizEquity

The BizEquity valuation tool is far ahead of its competitors. It offers:

1. Accuracy and breadth of range
2. Quantity and diversity of company types served (throughout a firm's life-cycle)
3. User-friendliness, visual appeal and capability to save/update appraisals
4. Expanded income, asset and liability coverage, with Hints and Learn More options for the user
5. Initial contributions to the BizEquity™ Online Valuation Library and Blog Collection
6. Interactivity based on the business owner's ability to engage in sensitivity analysis, with real-time feedback regarding business value
7. Number of overall industries covered, and a dynamic search functionality – real-time industry analysis comes up as you type in your industry
8. Holistic life-cycle valuation methodology, which shows where you are in your business journey.

The first and last key offerings give the business owner information about how their business value will change, and the business valuation will change as the business evolves.

Earnings and cash flow can be accurately and fairly recorded to be useful estimates of fair market or liquidation value. The standard valuation principles and procedures are based on those used by professional appraisers.

For many types of companies, last year's revenues and profits are rarely an accurate indication of the dynamic revenue opportunities the future may hold. By definition, historical measures of return can't accurately gauge the impact of that management plans involving new products or services or cost savings plans or synergistic mergers will have on company value. It is always necessary to keep an eye on the future when it comes to holistic business valuation. It's a cornerstone of modern financial theory that the value of any asset (or collection of assets) is the 'risk-adjusted, net present value' of all future cash flows.

In the future, most companies will evolve from 'the idea' to 'the product' to 'revenue and product growth' to 'margin growth' to 'maturation' and then 'decline' as the life cycle unfolds.

Growth can be negative for the first time, causing the firm to sell less productive assets or otherwise downsize. The company may be generating returns below the cost of capital.

The possibility of failure (insolvency or bankruptcy) emerges for the first time, especially for pursuing new core markets. Underfunded pensions and various legal claims can suppress market value substantially. The set of liquidity preferences will affect equity value of all types.

The BizEquity valuation will guide a business owner through all of the stages of their entrepreneurial journey.

We estimate the cost of the BizEquity solution is 1/25th the cost of the average offline business valuation service, and is produced in 1/25,000th of the time.

We believe that universal access to this service will educate business owners, and help them understand if and when they need a more formal appraisal report.

We offer more than just a valuation number or even valuation report; we are offering to educate the entrepreneur about the **principles of business valuation** and how they can use this knowledge to make the most of their most precious asset.

What to do next

In 1908, a Norwegian industrialist bought a beautiful oil painting, *Sunset at Montmajour*, which he believed to be by Vincent van Gogh.

Unfortunately, someone he thought knew their stuff suggested it was either a fake or wrongly attributed.

As a result, it was stuffed out of sight, in his attic. He died in 1970, convinced that he had been taken for a ride. Today, however, new research suggests it is indeed a van Gogh painting, and it recently sold for $34.7 million (£23m).

In many ways, a small business owner is like this industrialist. Because the painting was not properly identified and given its true value, he was not able to value it, artistically or financially.

BizEquity believes that valuations change lives. Small businesses – the greatest assets within an economy – are being devalued by big business, by governments, and by each other, and we believe that a revolution in small business valuation will transform their position in the world.

After all if you don't value it, you can't value it.

If *you* want to get your business valued, and be in the most powerful position available to a business owner, go to BizEquity's website (www.bizequity.com) which will give you all you need to know about how to proceed with the most sensible step of your business life.

Enter the discount code WYBW to receive a discount on your valuation and be matched to our network of advisors.

Allow BizEquity to give you the information that will help you make the best of your business.

Glossary

Asset Sale (Asset Value): Includes *only* inventory or supplies, fixed assets and all intangible assets. It excludes all liquid financial assets and all liabilities, and the buyer operates from a newly-formed legal entity. In an asset sale, the seller keeps the cash and receivables, but delivers the business free and clear of all debt.

Black & Scholes option valuation formula: Introduced in 1973 by economists Fischer Black, Myron Scholes and Robert Merton, it is the most commonly-known options pricing model, by which the theoretical price of European options are calculated. As Nobel Prizes are not awarded posthumously, Scholes and Merton were awarded the 1997 Nobel Prize in Economics for this model, while Black was recognized and credited (*Investopedia.com*).

Big Data: Really small, purposed data insights on a particular sequence of questions or on a particular insight. According to SAS (*www.sas.com*), Big Data 'describes the large volume of data – both structured and unstructured – that inundates a business on a day-to-day basis. But it's not the amount of data that's important. It's what organizations do with the data that matters.'

Cash-to-Debt Over Time: Shows the ability of a company to pay off existing debts, and compares a company's operating cash balance to its total debt. This ratio provides an indication of the company's ability to cover total debt (both short- and long-term) with its operating cash holdings.

Cash Flow-to-Revenue Over Time: An indicator of a firm's ability to convert sales revenue into spendable cash for the ownership. It's often also a key measure when analysing a company's ability to grow without the assistance of capital.

Cost Approach: a valuation approach based on how much has been put into a business. A business owner would not wish to sell his or her business for less than the money he or she had invested.

Debt-to-Equity Over Time: Shows the extent of the company's debt load in comparison to its equity value. This solvency ratio is a function of the firm's capital structure (wherein all assets must be financed by either debt or equity), and provides a measure of the company's financial leverage.

Earnings Before Interest, Taxes, Depreciation, and Amortization (EBITDA): Typically used give an investor an indication as to how much a company is earning. EBITDA helps an investor assess what the return on investment can be if he or she does buy a company.

Enterprise Value: A reflection of the firm's value as a functioning entity. It facilitates the comparison of companies with varying levels of debt.

Equity Sale (Equity Value): Includes all fixed assets, intangible assets, and inventory or supplies, as well as liquid financial assets, but with all liabilities deducted. An equity sale involves a full transfer of the legal entity including all account balances and current tax attributes.

Fair Market Value: The most common standard of value that's based on a hypothetical buyer and seller, who are under no duress and engage in a full exchange of all information. It's the estimated price at which a fully-informed buyer and a fully-informed seller are free and willing to conduct the sale or transaction, and is typically the basis for valuations for tax purposes, whereas business acquisitions are often valued from the perspective of investment value.

Fixed Assets-to-Income Over Time: Provides insight into the firm's profitability relative to its stock of fixed assets (e.g. furniture, fixtures and equipment/vehicles).

Fixed Assets Turnover Over Time: An activity ratio that refers to the productivity of a company's assets. It shows the company's ability to generate net sales from its investments in fixed assets.

Going Concern: A business enterprise with ongoing operations.

Income Approach: a valuation approach based on what the business is earning.

Income-to-Revenue Over Time: Also known as 'return on sales'; indicates the relative profit margin of the company for each dollar of sales. A rising percentage will often lead to a higher valuation.

Inventory Turnover Over Time: Refers to how long it takes to sell inventory on hand. This activity or turnover ratio identifies how efficiently goods are sold, by calculating how many times a company's inventory is sold and replaced in a given time period.

Interest Coverage Over Time: Also referred to as 'times interest earned', this shows how much cushion a company has in paying its interest expenses. This solvency ratio is equal to Earnings Before Interest and Taxes (EBIT) divided by interest expense, and it is used to determine the ease by which a company can pay interest on outstanding debt obligations.

Inventory-to-Income Over Time: Illustrates the relative importance of inventory holdings (typically carried at lower cost or market) to company profitability.

Investment Value: Also known as the value to a specific or known purchaser.

Liquidation Value: The net amount that would be realized if the business is terminated and the assets sold piecemeal.

Market Approach: A valuation approach based on the strategic market value the market is willing to tolerate, a perceived projected value, and revenue. It seeks to transform measures of profits or cash flow into estimates of value through multiples, capitalization rates and discount rates.

Receivables-to-Income Over Time: Provides an indication of the amount of credit granted to the customer base, relative to ongoing profits.

Receivables (Conversion) Over Time: The number of days it takes a company to collect its accounts receivables. An increase over time could signal difficulty in collecting from customers.

Return on Equity (RoE) Over Time: The amount of net income generated as a percentage of shareholder's equity. RoE measures a company's profitability by depicting how much profit a company generates with the money shareholders have, and is also an indication of the strength of the business model.

Sellers Discretionary Earnings (SDE): Generally used for evaluating businesses with gross annual sales under $1,000,000. For larger business, EBITDA is more frequently used.

Standard of Value: Refers to the type of value conclusion generated during a business valuation.

Time Value of Money: A concept wherein an amount of money available today is worth more than the same amount of money expected further in the future, because of the earning capacity it holds.

Total Debt-to-Income Over Time: The relationship between total company obligations at any point in time (short- and long-term debt) and on-going profit performance.

The Authors

Michael Carter is the CEO of BizEquity and the inventor of the market-leading online valuation service that is helping the small business economy. Mike has been called one of the top 100 Financial Technology leaders globally by Hot Topics Media in London, and BizEquity was recently recognized as one of the top 360 companies in the United States by Entrepreneur Media. Prior to founding BizEquity, Mike was Managing Director of The Musser Group where he worked with legendary investor Warren V. 'Pete' Musser to invest in small businesses. Mike was one of the youngest executive officers ever of a billion-dollar public traded Internet Professional Services Company; founded the first dashboard software company called Dashboard Systems; and was one of the first to invent the 'virtual data warehousing' technology used in most Big Data applications today. He began his career at Cambridge Technology Partners in management consulting.

Daniel Priestley is a successful entrepreneur who has built and sold businesses in Australia, Singapore and the UK. He's the co-founder of Dent Global, which runs world-leading business accelerators and events for growing enterprises. With offices in the UK, USA, Singapore and Australia, Dent works with over 1000 entrepreneurs and business leaders each year to develop their business, and is endorsed by the Institute of Leadership and Management. Daniel is the author of the best-selling books *Key Person of Influence*, *Entrepreneur Revolution* and *Oversubscribed*.

Scott Gabehart is the Chief Valuation Officer of BizEquity, and a Certified Business Appraiser through the Institute of Business Appraisers at his firm, Gabehart Valuation Services. He has evaluated, appraised and sold over 3,000 businesses since 1992. Specializing in SBA business appraisals on behalf of many lenders across the United States, his experience includes work in areas such as bankruptcy, estate and gift taxation, ESOP formation and administration, matrimonial dissolution, partnership disputes and transaction/strategic planning. He is the author of the seminal work in the market, *The Business Valuation Book*.

CPSIA information can be obtained
at www.ICGtesting.com
Printed in the USA
BVHW08s0026200918
527808BV00005B/6/P